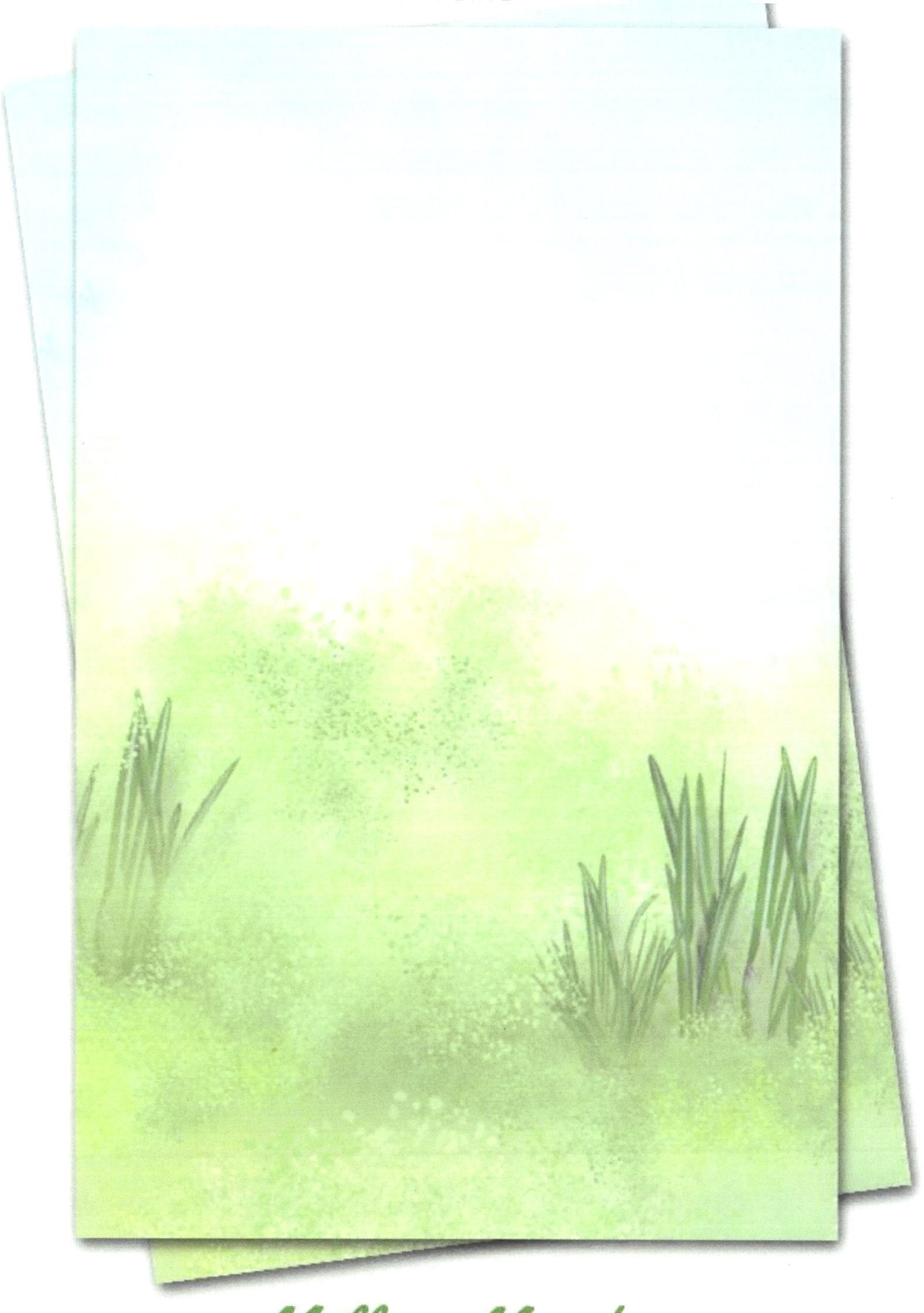

Mellow Meadow

STATIONERY PAPER

25 SHEETS | 5.5" x 8.5" | Half-Letter Size Paper | Simply Cut Out & Use

Simply Cut Out & Use

Simply Cut Out & Use

Simply Cut Out & Use

Simply Cut Out & Use

Simply Cut Out & Use

Simply Cut Out & Use

Simply Cut Out & Use

Simply Cut Out & Use

Simply Cut Out & Use

Simply Cut Out & Use

Simply Cut Out & Use

Simply Cut Out & Use

Simply Cut Out & Use

Simply Cut Out & Use

Simply Cut Out & Use

Simply Cut Out & Use

Simply Cut Out & Use

Simply Cut Out & Use

Simply Cut Out & Use

Simply Cut Out & Use

Simply Cut Out & Use

Simply Cut Out & Use